THE AMAZING BOOK C

GW01246762

AROUND THE
WORLD

for being the co-founding member of the laziest writing group in history. Emma Phelan for setting the world ablaze. This book is coming out twenty years to the day since I met you. I love that. I love it so much. Liz Phillips for your helpful and often hilarious feedback on my poems. Lee-Anne Poole for your wit and tenderness and also your writing, which is among my favourite. Scandalnavia for shaping me and my art making to this day. Lou Sheppard, for that donut and the infinite love and support. You are the moon in my sky. Anne Simpson, it was an honour to have you edit this book. Zanette Singh for the breakfasts, laughs, cigarettes, and love over so many years, but especially that one. Karen Solie, your feedback helped so many of these poems take a shape I'm proud of. Ocean Vuong, workshopping with you had such a profound effect on my writing. Zoe Whittall for all your support and being an inspiration for what seems like forever. Beth Wilson for so much, but especially getting that huntsman on Central Ave. Erin Wunker and Bart Vautour for tenderness and dinners in tough times. Also, to all the poets whose feedback in workshops has shaped these poems. Working with you was a privilege.

My Faeroese family, who so often put a roof over my head when I write, especially Leila, Daddi, Høgni, Annika, Christina, Jørgin, and Margreta.

To all my wonderful friends, crushes, and other queers who populated my twenties and thirties, you are in these pages. You are in my heart. There is far too many of you to name, but I am grateful to you always.

THE AMAZING BOOK OF FIRSTS

AROUND THE WORLD

Written by David Smith & Sue Cassin
Illustrated by Kim Blundell & Kate Davies

Edited by Catriona Macgregor

COLLINS

CONTENTS

EXPLORERS AND DISCOVERERS
p. 22-23

A collection of daring first-time explorations, including the first journeys made across North America, Africa and Australia.

MOUNTAINS
p. 24-25

The first people to climb Everest, the first people to reach the mountains of the Moon, plus many other mountaineering moments!

COUNTRIES
p. 26-27

The first banana-shaped stamp, the first driving test, the first artificial rain and other unique firsts from different countries.

MISCELLANEOUS
p. 28-29

An amazing selection of one-off firsts, such as the first lift, the first wedding ring and the first motorized doctor!

ROAD TRAVEL

PETROL-POWERED CAR—
The first petrol-driven car
was made in 1885 by Karl
Benz of Germany. It was
the 'Motorwagen' model,
and could travel at a speed
of 16km per hour.

PEDAL-PUSHER—The first bicycle was
built in 1839 by Kirkpatrick MacMillan
of Great Britain. It was called a 'velocipede',
and had pedals attached to rods, which
turned the back wheel.

NEW BUS ROUTE—The first
petrol-engined bus was a
five-horse-power single-
decker. It began running on
a fifteen-km route in North
Rhineland, West Germany
in 1895.

MOTORCYCLE PATENT—The first
motorcycle was patented in 1868 by Ernest
and Pierre Michaux of France. It was a
bicycle powered by a small steam engine,
which was fitted behind the saddle.

AMBULANCE EXHIBITION

—The first motor ambulance had a Daimler engine and was built by Réné Panhard and Emile Levassor. It was exhibited in Paris in December 1895.

MONO-WHEEL MADNESS

—A Mr Christie, from the USA, designed the first mono-wheel—a very strange-looking motorized cycle. It consisted of a giant wheel fitted below with a powerful aircraft engine, which drove a chain to turn the axle. The brave motorist sat in the centre of the wheel just above the axle. Although the results of Christie's test drive are not recorded, he claimed that the vehicle could reach astonishing speeds of up to 400km per hour!

ARMY TRANSPORT

—In 1940 Karl Pabst designed the first jeep. It was specially produced for the US Army, and, during the Second World War, more than 649,000 models were manufactured.

SEA TRAVEL

FULL STEAM AHEAD—The first large iron steamship was the *SS Great Britain*, designed by Isambard Kingdom Brunel of England in 1843. The ship left Liverpool in July 1845 on her maiden voyage to New York, carrying 60 passengers and almost 70,000kg of cargo. The journey took just less than fifteen full days.

RECORD BREAKER—The first real clipper ship was called the *Sea Witch* and was designed by an American called John Griffiths. The ship was first launched in 1849 and created an all-time record in taking only 74 days, 14 hours to sail from China to New York.

ATLANTIC CROSSING—The first steamship to cross the Atlantic was a 320-tonne paddle-wheeler called the *Savannah*, in 1819. Despite running out of fuel off the coast of Ireland, it took the ship 27 days, 11 hours to reach Liverpool, completing her journey by sail.

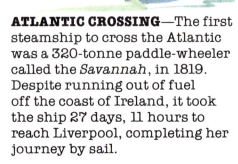

SUBMARINE SUCCESS—In 1955 the first nuclear-powered submarine, *Nautilus*, made its sea trial. In its first 2 years it cruised a distance of 99,800km without ever refuelling, but used no more than 3.6kg of uranium.

PLAIN SAILING—In September 1519 the *Vittoria* left Spain to sail round the world. She successfully completed her voyage in September 1522, having covered a distance of 49,400km, and became the first ship ever to travel right round the globe.

FLOATING ON AIR—By 1959 Sir Christopher Cockerell of Great Britain had developed the first hovercraft. It was the SR. N1, and floated on a cushion of air. It was this hovercraft which, in July 1962, provided the first regular passenger-carrying service— from Rhyl in North Wales to Wallasey in North West England.

CAR CARRIER FIRST—The first ship designed specially for carrying cars was the *Opama Mara*, built in Japan in 1965. She could carry as many as 1,200 at once.

RAIL TRAVEL

EARLY LOCOMOTIVE—The first steam locomotive began running in 1804 near Merthyr Tydfil in South Wales. It was built by Richard Trevithick and travelled at an average speed of 8km per hour on the 16km-long track, but it broke the plate rails.

TRAIN TRAVEL FIRST—The first modern railway service operated entirely by steam locomotives was the Liverpool to Manchester Railway, built by George Stevenson and his son, Robert. The track was 50km long and opened for the first time on 15 September 1830.

TOP SPEED TRAIN—The first high-speed diesel train was called *The Flying Hamburger*. In 1932 it ran between Hamburg and Berlin at speeds of over 161km per hour.

CITY'S SHOW PIECE—In 1876 the first passenger-carrying monorail was built in Fairmount Park, Philadelphia, by General Roy Stone. It was constructed as part of Philadelphia's centenary exhibition.

FIRST CLASS DINER—

In 1863 passengers journeying between Philadelphia and Baltimore were the first to be able to dine whilst travelling in a train. Two ordinary coaches were fitted with an eating bar, dining tables and chairs, and were decorated in the manner of a first class restaurant.

GOING UNDERGROUND—

The Metropolitan Railway in London was opened to passengers in 1863. It was 6.4km long and was the first underground passenger railway ever. On the first day 30,000 people journeyed on the coaches, which were pulled along by a steam locomotive.

AIR TRAVEL

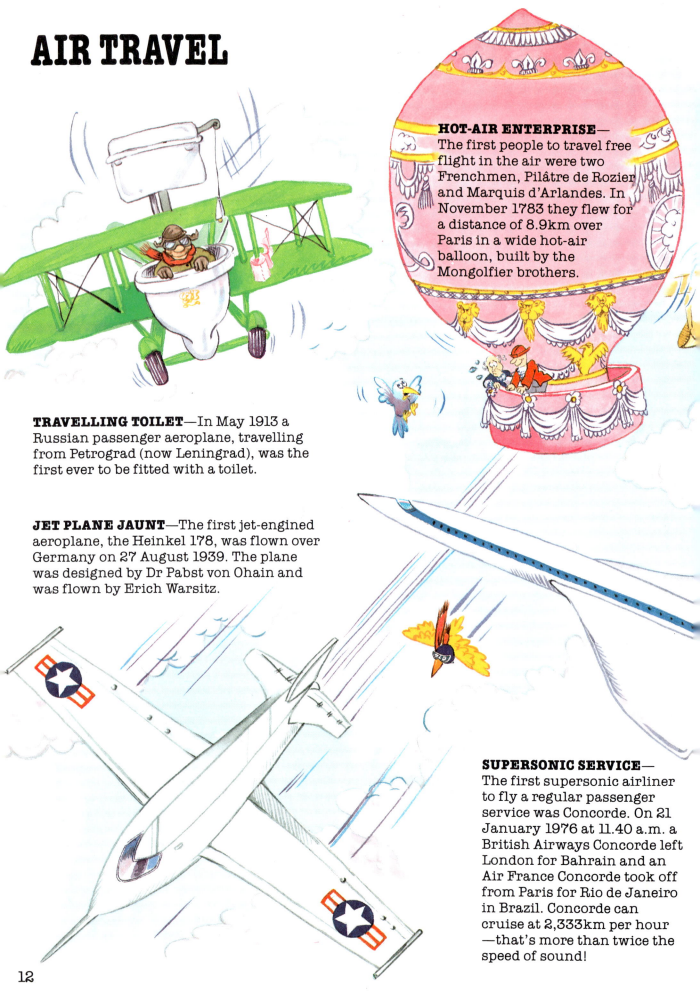

HOT-AIR ENTERPRISE—
The first people to travel free flight in the air were two Frenchmen, Pilâtre de Rozier and Marquis d'Arlandes. In November 1783 they flew for a distance of 8.9km over Paris in a wide hot-air balloon, built by the Mongolfier brothers.

TRAVELLING TOILET—In May 1913 a Russian passenger aeroplane, travelling from Petrograd (now Leningrad), was the first ever to be fitted with a toilet.

JET PLANE JAUNT—The first jet-engined aeroplane, the Heinkel 178, was flown over Germany on 27 August 1939. The plane was designed by Dr Pabst von Ohain and was flown by Erich Warsitz.

SUPERSONIC SERVICE—
The first supersonic airliner to fly a regular passenger service was Concorde. On 21 January 1976 at 11.40 a.m. a British Airways Concorde left London for Bahrain and an Air France Concorde took off from Paris for Rio de Janeiro in Brazil. Concorde can cruise at 2,333km per hour —that's more than twice the speed of sound!

FAST FLIGHT—In October 1947 Captain Charles Yeager of the USA piloted a Bell X-1 rocket-powered plane at a speed of Mach 1.015 (1,078km per hour)—this was the first supersonic flight.

HIJACKED AIRLINE—The first aeroplane to be hijacked was the Cathay Pacific Airways flying-boat *Miss Macao*. In June 1948 it was seized by a gang of Chinese bandits shortly after taking off from Macao, on a flight to Hong Kong.

FIRST AIR HOSTESS—Ellen Church, a registered nurse from Iowa, was the first air hostess. On 15 May 1930 she welcomed her first passengers aboard a United Airlines Boeing 80A aircraft at Oakland Airport in the United States.

SPACE FLIGHTS

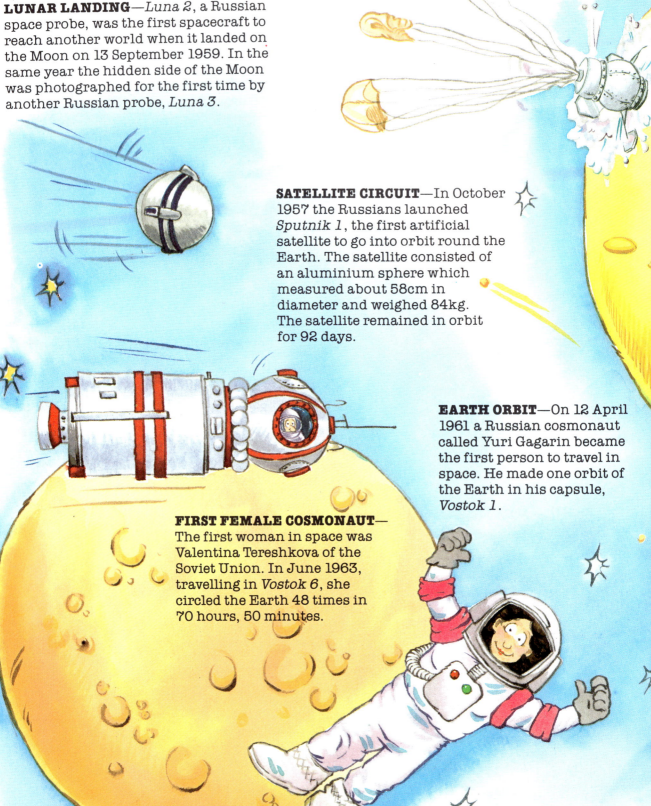

LUNAR LANDING—*Luna 2*, a Russian space probe, was the first spacecraft to reach another world when it landed on the Moon on 13 September 1959. In the same year the hidden side of the Moon was photographed for the first time by another Russian probe, *Luna 3*.

SATELLITE CIRCUIT—In October 1957 the Russians launched *Sputnik 1*, the first artificial satellite to go into orbit round the Earth. The satellite consisted of an aluminium sphere which measured about 58cm in diameter and weighed 84kg. The satellite remained in orbit for 92 days.

EARTH ORBIT—On 12 April 1961 a Russian cosmonaut called Yuri Gagarin became the first person to travel in space. He made one orbit of the Earth in his capsule, *Vostok 1*.

FIRST FEMALE COSMONAUT—The first woman in space was Valentina Tereshkova of the Soviet Union. In June 1963, travelling in *Vostok 6*, she circled the Earth 48 times in 70 hours, 50 minutes.

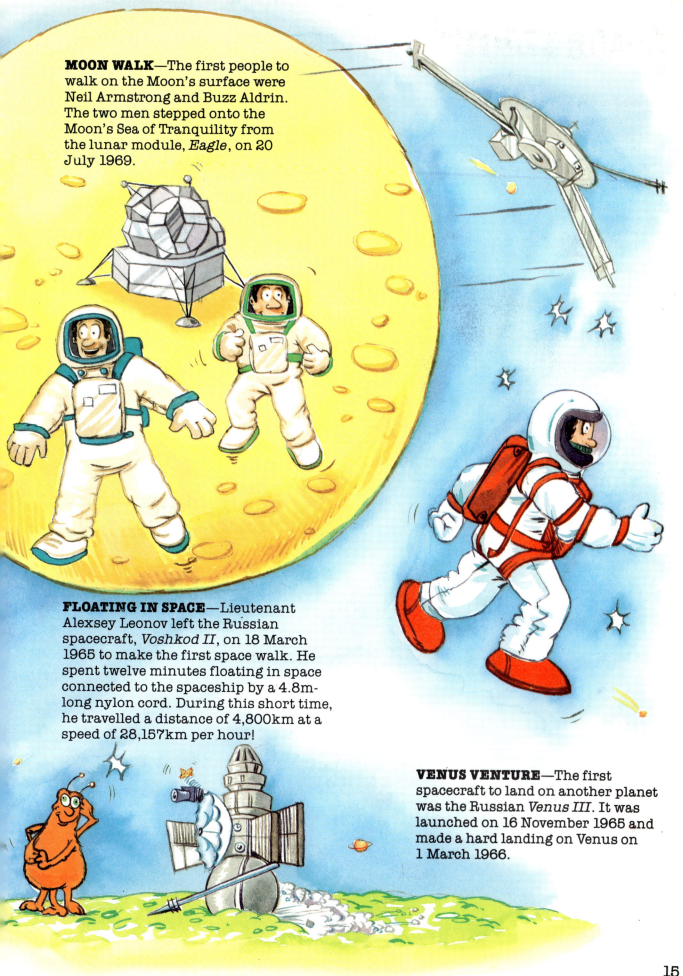

MOON WALK—The first people to walk on the Moon's surface were Neil Armstrong and Buzz Aldrin. The two men stepped onto the Moon's Sea of Tranquility from the lunar module, *Eagle*, on 20 July 1969.

FLOATING IN SPACE—Lieutenant Alexsey Leonov left the Russian spacecraft, *Voshkod II*, on 18 March 1965 to make the first space walk. He spent twelve minutes floating in space connected to the spaceship by a 4.8m-long nylon cord. During this short time, he travelled a distance of 4,800km at a speed of 28,157km per hour!

VENUS VENTURE—The first spacecraft to land on another planet was the Russian *Venus III*. It was launched on 16 November 1965 and made a hard landing on Venus on 1 March 1966.

UNDERWATER FIRSTS

AQUALUNG INVENTION—
The aqualung was used for
the first time during the
Second World War. It was a
complete breathing set for
deep-sea diving and was
produced by Jacques
Cousteau, a serving officer in
the French Navy, and Emile
Gagnan, a French engineer.

DARING DIVE—In January 1960 Jacques
Piccard, a Swiss scientist, and Lieutenant
Donald Walsh, of the US Navy, made the first
dive in a bathyscaphe. They descended to the
deepest part of the Pacific Ocean—10,917m—
in the *Trieste*. The descent took them a total
of 4 hours, 48 minutes.

DEEP-SEA OBSERVATION—The
bathysphere was first built by
William Beebe and Otis Barton of
the USA. The first dive was made
off the coast of Bermuda in June
1930, and four years later they
were the first to descend to a
depth of more than 912m.

FROG'S FEET—Frogman flippers were
first designed in 1927 by Louis de Corlieu.

AMAZING FEAT—The first reference to a diving bell was in 1538 in Toledo in Spain. Apparently, two Greeks climbed into a large inverted 'kettle' in which a lamp burned. The 'kettle' was lowered into the water and when it was brought to the surface again, the watching crowd was amazed to see that the clothes of the two Greeks were still dry, and that the lamp was still burning!

UNDERWATER FILMS—The first successful underwater movie pictures were taken in the 1930s by a Mr Williamson of the USA. The pictures were taken in clear waters off the coast of Florida.

SUBTERRANEAN TELEVISION—Underwater television cameras were first used in 1954 when search teams were looking for the wreckage of a Comet airliner which crashed into the Mediterranean Sea off the island of Elba.

DIVING SUIT DESIGN—The first diving suit was invented in 1837 by Augustus Siebe of London. The general design, apart from additions of new technology, is still in use today.

POLAR FIRSTS

POLAR BREAKTHROUGH—In August 1977 the Russian nuclear icebreaker, *Arktika*, became the first ship to succeed in breaking through the polar ice and reach the North Pole.

LONELY JOURNEY—A Japanese explorer called Naomi Uemera was the first person to reach the North Pole travelling alone. He arrived there on 1 May 1978, on a sledge drawn by seventeen huskies.

CHILLY CROSSING—The first crossing of the Arctic sea-ice was achieved by the British Trans-Arctic Expedition led by Wally Herbert in 1969. The 4,699km journey took 464 days.

CONTINENT TREK—The first surface crossing of the Antarctic continent was completed on 2 March 1958 after a 99- day trek of 3,473km. The party of twelve was led by Sir Vivian Fuchs of Great Britain.

TEAM ACHIEVEMENT—
In April 1909 an American,
Robert Peary, and his small
team were the first to reach
the North Pole.

On 16 December 1911, after
a 53-day march with dog
sledges, a Norwegian party
led by Roald Amundsen
finally arrived at the South
Pole. They were the first
people ever to achieve this.

FROSTY FLIGHTS—On
9 May 1926 Commander
Richard Byrd of the USA
made the first flight ever
over the North Pole. He
made his journey in a
Fokker aeroplane.

In November 1929
Commander Byrd was a
member of the four-man
crew of a Ford Trimotor
plane which made the first
flight over the South Pole.

CIRCLE VOYAGE—In January 1773 Captain
James Cook R.N. of Great Britain and his
crew of 118 men were the first to cross the
Antarctic Circle. They made their journey in
a 462-tonne vessel called the *Resolution*.

CIRCUMNAVIGATING THE GLOBE

GLOBE TROTTING—The first person to walk right round the world was David Kunst of the USA. It took him from 10 June 1970 until 5 October 1974 to complete his mammoth trek.

LONG-DISTANCE DRIVE—Garry Sowerby and Ken Langley from Canada were the first people to drive round the Earth in a car in less than 75 days. Driving a Volvo 245 DL, they left Toronto on 6 September 1980 and motored through four continents and 23 countries, covering an overall distance of 43,030km.

UNDERWATER VOYAGE—The American submarine, the *Triton*, was the first to travel round the world underwater. On 16 February 1960 Captain Edward Beach and a crew of 182 left New England and returned on 10 May 1960, having travelled a distance of 49,422km.

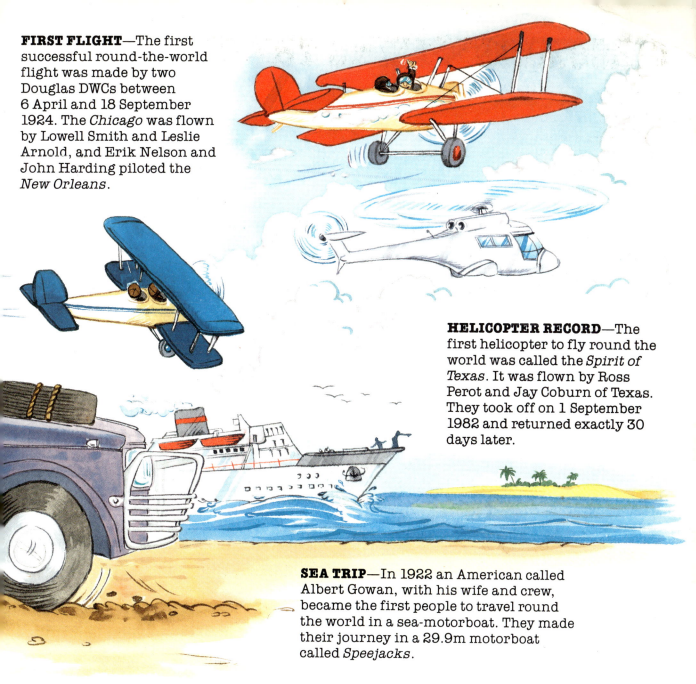

FIRST FLIGHT—The first successful round-the-world flight was made by two Douglas DWCs between 6 April and 18 September 1924. The *Chicago* was flown by Lowell Smith and Leslie Arnold, and Erik Nelson and John Harding piloted the *New Orleans*.

HELICOPTER RECORD—The first helicopter to fly round the world was called the *Spirit of Texas*. It was flown by Ross Perot and Jay Coburn of Texas. They took off on 1 September 1982 and returned exactly 30 days later.

SEA TRIP—In 1922 an American called Albert Gowan, with his wife and crew, became the first people to travel round the world in a sea-motorboat. They made their journey in a 29.9m motorboat called *Speejacks*.

DANGEROUS JOURNEY—The first people ever to travel right round the globe were the crew of a sailing ship called the *Vittoria*. In September 1519 a Portuguese navigator, Ferdinand Magellan, led five ships from Spain intending to sail round the world. Unfortunately, Magellan was killed by natives in the Philippines, and the *Vittoria* was the only vessel to complete the journey. Of the 270 men who set out on the voyage, only 31 survived and returned to Spain.

EXPLORERS AND DISCOVERERS

CANADIAN QUEST—In 1534 Jacques Cartier, a French explorer, crossed the Atlantic and was the first European to explore Canada. He gave the country its name after hearing a similar word used to describe an Indian village.

COAST TO COAST—A Scottish-born Canadian called Sir Alexander Mackenzie was the first explorer to cross the full breadth of North America. He and his party set out from Fort Chipewyan on Lake Athabasca in Canada and arrived at Cape Menzies on the Pacific Coast in July 1793.

FOOD SHORTAGE—In 1860 Robert O'Hara Burke and William Wills succeeded in making the first South to North crossing of Australia from Victoria to the Gulf of Carpentaria. However, on their return journey they ran out of food and, sadly, did not survive.

FORBIDDEN LANDING—Abel Janszoon Tasman, a Dutch explorer, was the first European explorer to reach New Zealand. He arrived in 1642, but unfortunately the Maoris would not let him land!

VIKING VENTURE—A Viking called Leif Erikson was the first explorer to discover North America. In about AD 1000 he landed in Newfoundland.

SURPRISE LANDING— In 1492 Christopher Columbus discovered three islands of the West Indies —the Bahamas, Haiti and Cuba. He thought that he had landed in or near India, which is why this group of islands is called the West Indies.

AFRICAN CROSSING—A British-American explorer, Sir Henry Morton Stanley was the first to travel across Africa from East to West. He left Zanzibar in November 1874 and 999 days later he arrived at the mouth of the River Congo.

AMAZON ADVENTURE—In 1499 Vincente Pinzon from Portugal discovered Brazil and the River Amazon. Today, Brazil is the only country on the American Continent where Portugese is the official language.

MOUNTAINS

MOUNTAIN RECORD—On 29 May 1953 Edmund Hillary and Sherpa Tenzing became the first people to climb to the summit of Mount Everest.

ALPINE ASCENT—The first organized Alpine climb was made by a geologist, Jacques Balmat, and a doctor, Michel Paccard. They climbed Mont Blanc, the highest mountain in the Alps (4,807m), in 1786.

MOUNTAIN CONQUEROR—Richard Bass of the USA was the first person to climb the highest mountains in each of the seven continents. He climbed Kilimanjaro in Africa, Vinson Massif in Antarctica, El'brus in Europe, McKinley in North America, Aconcagua in South America, and Kosciusko in Australia. In 1985 he completed the last of his climbs with his conquest of Mount Everest in Asia.

MOON MOUNTAINS—The first people to reach the summit of the highest mountains on the Moon—the Descartes Mountains (7,830m)—were two American astronauts, Captain Young and Major Dukes, in April 1972.

VOLCANO VENTURE—In July 1986 Teiichi Igarushi of Japan became the first person to climb to the top of Mount Fujiyama, a 3,776m extinct volcano and the highest peak in Japan.

MOUNTAIN CITY—The first and only capital city in the world situated at an altitude of over 3,630m is La Paz in Bolivia. The city lies in the Andes Mountains.

KING'S ORDERS—The first person to have climbed a mountain on royal command was Antoine de Ville in 1492. King Charles VIII of France ordered him to take a party of guests to the top of Mont Aiguille, a 2,097m peak near Grenoble.

COUNTRIES

WHITE CHRISTMAS—Las Vegas, a gambling and entertainment city in the Nevada Desert, had snow for the first time ever on Christmas Day, 1988.

FUNNY FLAG—The first and only flag to have different designs on either side, is that of Paraguay, in South America.

BANANA STAMP—In 1974 Tonga became the first country to issue a postage stamp shaped like a banana!

BADGER SAFETY—The first motorway underpass built specially for badgers, was constructed under the M5 motorway near Exeter in the south of England.

ARTIFICIAL WEATHER—Israel was the first country to have an artificial rainfall. In 1984 Professor Gagin and a team of scientists bombarded clouds with a fine powder of iodine filings, causing rain to fall.

FIRST DRIVING TEST—The first country to introduce motor car driving tests was France. The very first test was taken in 1893 in Paris.

AEROSOL BAN—In 1978 Sweden was the first country to ban aerosols containing CFCs (chlorofluorocarbons), which have a harmful effect on the Earth's ozone layer.

SILVER SHOWER—In June 1940, Gorky in the USSR was the first place to have silver coins showered upon it. A tornado uncovered an old chest full of coins, lifted it into the air and dropped more than 1,000 coins on the village!

MISCELLANEOUS

BRAVERY AWARD—The laurel wreath was the first decoration for bravery, and was awarded by the Ancient Greeks and Romans. Julius Caesar, the great Roman general, wore a laurel wreath most of the time to hide his bald head!

SECRET MEETING—The first lift was installed in the Palace of Versailles, France, in 1743. It was used only by King Louis XV to enable him to visit his lover, Madame de Châteauroux, on the floor above. The lift was worked by ropes and pulleys and was on the outside of the building, not inside as most lifts are today.

MOTORIZED DOCTOR—In 1895 Dr Carlos Booth of Youngstown, Ohio was the first doctor to use a motor car for visiting his patients. However, he used the car for only eighteen months because riders complained that it upset their horses.

INDIAN RUBBER—The first people to play with rubber balls were the Maya Indians, who lived in Central America nearly 1,000 years ago.

VALUABLE BIRDS—The Incas of South America were the first to realize the tremendous value of two Peruvian birds —the booby and the cormorant, which feed on anchovies and other small fish. These birds were placed under strict protection because their droppings are said to make the finest fertilizer in the world!

TOKEN OF LOVE—The Ancient Egyptians were the first people to wear wedding rings. In their written language (hieroglyphics) its shape meant 'for ever'.

The Romans believed that there was a nerve which ran directly from the heart to the third finger of the left hand. This is why it is the custom in many countries today to wear the wedding ring on that finger.

INDEX